Tea *with* *Patsy Clairmont*

Tea *with* Patsy Clairmont

Patsy Clairmont
Janet Kobobel Grant, Contributing Editor

A CROSSINGS BOOK CLUB EDITION

Published by Servant Publications
P.O. Box 8617
Ann Arbor, Michigan 48107

Contributing Editor: Janet Kobobel Grant
Editor: Gwen Ellis
Art Director: Diane Bareis
Photography: Bob Foran, Ann Arbor, MI
Cover design: BC Studios, Colorado Springs, CO

97 98 99 00 10 9 8 7 6 5 4 3 2 1

Printed in Mexico.

*To Danya,
my darling daughter-in-law, who is my cup of tea.*

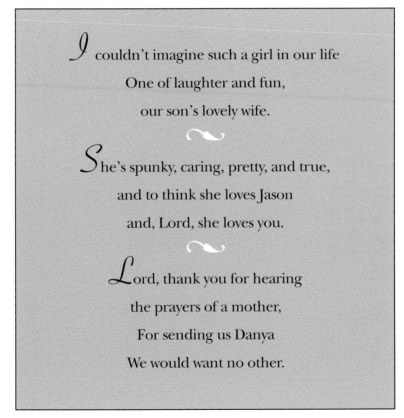

I couldn't imagine such a girl in our life

One of laughter and fun,

our son's lovely wife.

*S*he's spunky, caring, pretty, and true,

and to think she loves Jason

and, Lord, she loves you.

*L*ord, thank you for hearing

the prayers of a mother,

For sending us Danya

We would want no other.

Contents

~

Tea Time

~

What is there about a cup of tea that charms a woman's heart? I believe tea is much more than an amber liquid to be sipped. It also speaks of a different pace, a genteel space, a still moment, a quiet thought, and a worthy conversation. Tea is another mind-set, one very different from the intensely driven whirl we live in. Tea time invites us to relax and to reflect; it helps us not to lose touch with ourselves and with others. And it permits us to unplug from our harriedness to nurture our souls.

Tea also whispers a language of romance, the romance of embracing loveliness. A graceful cup, a crocheted napkin, a sterling spoon, a lace doily, and a tea service help to establish a gentle ambiance. Our senses are soothed by a carefully prepared tea environment.

Tea is a sip of yesterday when times were less frantic and more family, when Polly put her kettle on, and we all had tea. Listen … can you hear the sounds of loved ones as they congregate around the comforting cups? The steaming kettle sings for attention as friends lean in to touch one another's lives.

My yesterdays are filled with the delicate sound of clinking ice cubes in tall glasses of sweet tea on hot summer days. The heat in the South was made more tolerable and more sociable by partaking of this delightful refreshment. In the noonday sun, we sought refuge on the shady porch and there drank our tea and enjoyed each other's company. These memories are even sweeter than was the tea.

Most importantly for me, teatime is when I collect myself before re-entering my passionate pursuits. This personal interlude becomes as sacred as a tête-à-tête with the One who understands my franticness, my longings, and my leanings. He reminds me that "in quietness and trust is your strength" (Isaiah 30:15b).

Partake with me some amber warmth, a cup of cheer, a sip of encouragement … and moments worth remembering.

Tea and Thee

Graceful china cup

Sterling silver spoon

Devotions set apart

My heart to His attune.

Time in His presence

Sips of English tea

Moments to remember

His great love for me.

Trifles

❧

My dictionary thinks a trifle is something of little importance. I have found, though, that little, inconsequential things can add up to memorable occasions. My friend Nancy and I are triflers. Not that we don't count—we enjoy little, playful pursuits as well as bigger, profound ones. When I stay at her home or she visits mine, we have delightful times that border on decadent.

For instance, we often have tea parties in her parlor. Nancy prepares scones as we chat and giggle. Then we cozy into her grandmother's Victorian sofa with our steaming cups of tea to discuss important issues—like the value of being a grandma (she is one; I'm not … yet). Our talk ranges from the mundane to the magnificent, from tips on sales to insights from Scripture. We try to cover it all.

On our tea-filled day, we also incorporate a truffle or two (or three). And even though a truffle is really quite a trifle, we can hardly wait to partake. Our agenda for the day also includes

Nancy's manicurist, who comes to her home and give us pedicures, sometimes prior to tea, sometimes afterwards. De-ca-dent!

One time, to extend our enjoyment of our tea party, we attended a symphony. The San Francisco Davies Symphony Hall was the exquisite setting for listening to the music of Berg, Schumann, Liadov, and Tchaikovsky.

When we get together, another part of our treat to each other is gift-giving. Often our gifts reflect our interest in tea. Books, accessories, bookmarks, and miniature tea sets keep us both oohing and ahhing. Since we live far apart, we stay in touch by reading the same devotional, sending cards (often with girls and tea parties depicted on them), and, once in a while, indulging in some long-distance giggle breaks.

It's probably just as well that we don't live too close. Decadent living can kill you. But what a way to go!

Twin Pots

On an antique shopping excursion, my friend Carol spotted a teapot with an illustration of two girls holding hands painted on it. She purchased it for me. Several months later, while once again browsing for treasures, Carol discovered a duplicate pot. This one, she bought for herself. Our twin pots have become a hallmark of our valued, forty-year friendship.

In many ways Carol and I are twin pots. (At this season, even our shapes are far more, shall we say, *pottish* looking than in our youth.) And we both spout off from time to time—but only with the warmest of intentions.

Carol and I have always enjoyed each other's company, and we share many common interests. We love to chatter about decorating, to study and critique art pieces, to discover antiques, to experience varied dining establishments (especially tea rooms), and to laugh until tears of joy leave us in soggy relief.

Through the years Carol and I have spent time away at cottages and bed and breakfast accommodations seeking solace and sanity from life's mercurial ways. At the end of such weeks, our husbands join us, and we conclude our adventure as a foursome.

Often Carol, an artist by trade, will sketch a picture of something in our new surroundings, and I will write a poem to go with the sketch. At a beautiful inn near Lake Michigan, I found myself drawn to a statue of a young boy playing a harp at the pool's edge beside a meadow. Carol captured the boy with her pencil. Then early one morning over breakfast tea I penned:

Meadow boy come out to play,

Symphony of breaking day.

Child of wonder, child of song,

To us alone this place belongs.

Harp of stone, hymn of praise,

noted songs in morning rays.

Sing to heaven songs of earth,

minstrel joy and floral mirth.

We tuck these sketches and poems into our journals as memory-enhancers for the time when we'll be too old to travel and we will be relegated to twin, motorized rocking chairs. These personal treasures help us to capture a sense of the places we have visited, the people we have met, and the lessons we have learned. And if we have figured out one thing in our journey, it's that life is full of lessons.

I am a lesson all by myself—I have several people I could refer you to who would confirm this. I have established a reputation for being a cracked pot. Carol, too, is a flawed pot, but we both long to be restored and used as worthy vessels. (Maybe even soothing teapots!) Our twin desire for restoration, linked with our willingness to own up to our weaknesses, has allowed us to come alongside each other and to offer a hand.

We have discovered that many women relate to feeling fragile and broken. Yet we girls (I love that youthful term) are finding we are strengthened when we are honest with each other and receive one another, cracks, chips, and all.

Carol and I know the worst and the best about each other. We are thrilled when one of us succeeds, and we are saddened when one of us experiences failure. We are committed to each other's best and leave room for those invariable times when we let the other down. We, like the twin pot girls, are determined to hold hands no matter how steamed we might become or how hot life's water may be.

Carol and I have dedicated ourselves to appreciating and applauding each other's talents, and to confessing our weakest traits to one another. This mutuality has taken us from the tea parlor, where we have shared in life, to the funeral parlor, where we have shared in death.

Three years ago, Carol's son Jeff died. I extended a hand of compassion, and we held on for dear life during the waves of grief. How precious we are to each other and how much we need one another!

Eventually Carol and I were able to leave the place of grief and re-enter the tea parlor. Sometimes our tea is mixed with tears and sometimes it is sweetened with memories. We are warmed by the tea and by the dear embrace of our friendship.

Tuxedo Tea Party

∾

Don't you love it when life takes you by sweet surprise? Like an unexpected laugh in the middle of a drama, these serendipitous moments breathe freshness back into our psyche and help us handle the next scene as it unfolds. More than once my serendipity has arrived at tea.

I've attended many Christian Booksellers Conventions, which are held annually in different parts of the country. During the week of the convention, I race from one publicity interview to another. I jaunt to breakfast, lunch, and dinner to tie up business and to touch base with long-lost friends. Add to that some public speaking, a stint at the autograph booth, and an authors' dinner, and the week becomes a dynamic, yet demanding, swirl of activity.

So when, at the last convention, I was invited to tea with friends from *Guideposts* magazine, I was interested yet reluctant. Would I have enough tread left on my Reeboks to rush to one more place? But the combination of tea and new friends was more temptation than I could resist; I added the event to my already bulging schedule.

Later, as I huffed and puffed my way to our rendezvous, I suspected I had taken on more in my week than I could handle. Just then, I spotted my tea friends Lenore, Gin, Terri, and Anna holding open the door to a white stretch limousine, which was ready to whisk us off to the restaurant.

"Hmm, yes, I do believe I can do this," I tittered to myself, feeling a fresh flow of strength.

When I slipped inside the limousine, it seemed endless. We giggled our way to the tea party, and by the time we arrived at the entrance of Thee White House Restaurant, the week's strain was already beginning to ease. My parched heart felt nurtured as I took in my friends' faces and the simple elegance of my surroundings.

Our white linen napkins were folded like tuxedo shirts encircled with heavy paper black bow ties. (These were actually calling cards for the restaurant. The address was printed on the reverse side.) We decided to order a potpourri of individual desserts with our tea. The gentlemen serving us were well-versed in both manners and menu, and they went out of their way to make this occasion memorable. The servers brought out chests of tea, described the flavors, and then set before each of us a steaming pot with our own private brew.

We commented on our tea selections, evaluating the myriad

flavors and aromas permeating our friendship circle. When our desserts arrived, we squealed (discreetly, of course), as polished black marble slabs were set before us with artistically placed desserts interspersed between ribbons and swirls of lovely sauces.

Once we had sufficiently drunk in our environment, we began to focus on each other. I asked the ladies, "What would you like to do when you grow up?" Soon we were chatting away, getting to know each other better in the short time allotted us.

Before we realized it, our tuxedo tea was over. It was time to disperse. We left with reluctance, and yet we were grateful that, in the midst of real life demands, we were able to sit, sip, and savor each other's company.

The tuxedo party was, for me, a joyous reprieve and a reminder that tea and friends are timeless treasures that revive and encourage the heart. I'm so pleased I didn't decline this invitation and miss a serendipi-tea.

Timeless Tea

❧

Whthen one enters the world of my friend Ruthann Bell, one takes a step back in time. Ruthann lives in an antique-appointed log home, handcasts her soaps, and passionately studies the Victorian era.

Throughout our relationship, we have shared, over steaming cups of tea, a range of emotions and dreams. Last year Ruthann decided that, instead of watching her hopes dissipate with the vapor from our teacups, she would vigorously pursue her longings. She left the professional world and opened her home as the Forest Farm Bed & Breakfast. She also developed Forest Farm Soaps made from the milk of the Toggenburg, Alpine, and Nubian goats she raises herself.

I admired Ruthann's choice since few of us have the gumption to step into our dreams, cinch them up like an old-fashioned corset, and wear them with dignity and pride. Most of us seem satisfied to speak of our wishes to one another and then traipse back into our usual routines convinced that dreams seldom come true. Ruthann's

FACING PAGE:
*Clustered around and upon my grandmother's icebox in my entry are
a nineteenth-century woman's finery she would have worn to a tea.*

decision to don her desires did cost her some personal conveniences—she had to give up some of her space to guests—but also earned her deep personal satisfaction.

As I've watched Ruthann, I've not only admired her courage, but I've also learned a bit about the deportment and the ways of a mid-1800s lady. Ruthann provided the replicas of bonnets and a tea dress from those days (meticulously stitched by her own hands) for the photo on the previous page. She also loaned me some of her female finery to display in my foyer. Included with the small items sitting atop my grandmother's ice box is an exquisite sterling silver cardholder in early Victorian filigree.

I am told that in the old days, a lady who stopped for tea and found you away would leave her calling card. It conveyed a twofold message: first, that she had attempted a visit, and second (and more importantly), that you now were expected to visit *her* for tea. A woman's heart was warmed to come home and find her pretty china or silver plate near the door filled with calling cards. It meant she was deemed an important part of the community's society.

A lady always wore gloves when she called on you, but removed them for tea itself. Her waist watch reminded her not to overstay her visit, as that was a sign of bad manners. (Actually, it still is.) A woman's broach became her traveling photo album. It allowed her the (silent) opportunity to display a treasured photograph of a family member without seeming braggadocio or forward.

At that time, high tea was more of a meal, while afternoon tea was more formal and delicate. Afternoon tea was a lady's mid-day activity providing light fare to sustain one between meals, and was offered in a tasteful social setting. It gave women an opportunity to exhibit their heirloom tea services and to exercise their punctilio.

After opening her bed and breakfast, Ruthann began to offer afternoon tea in her house. She hung a plaque by her front door that read "Mrs. Bell's Tea Parlor." I couldn't make reservations fast enough for myself and friends.

On the appointed afternoon Ann, Alicia, Carol, Diane, Karen, and I arrived at Forest Farm and were met at our vehicles by Mr. Bell dressed in Civil War-style attire. He ushered us into the parlor where we were greeted by Mrs. Bell (Ruthann).

On this hot, summer day, the open windows allowed a woodland breeze and floral scents from the surrounding gardens to fill the home with refreshing sweetness. Ruthann's floor-length servant's dress made the most lovely swishing sound as it rustled with her every move atop layers of crinolines. She welcomed us to her parlor and served us delicate, passion-fruit iced tea. That was soon followed by an array of tea sandwiches (chicken cashew, turkey with raspberry mayonnaise, and cucumbers with fresh herbs), sweet dainties, hot tea in china cups, and sterling spoons for stirring.

We toured her home, fussing over her timeless treasures. There were period spinning wheels, sewing machines, old family trunks, a pump organ, exquisite renaissance-revival and rococo furnishings, footed tubs, Civil War memorabilia, a small family gallery of her Welsh ancestors, and her extensive wardrobe of historically accurate Victorian dresses complete with vintage lace and ribbons.

We squealed with delight when Ruthann invited us each to select a vintage hat to wear into the parlor. Hats donned, we gathered around a velvet settee for photographs.

I was enthralled with our timeless tea party. It had reminded us of an era that encouraged femininity and genteel manners. I had had the distinct feeling, when I stepped into Mrs. Bell's parlor, that I had gone back to a special time in history. Mentally, I had slipped into Louisa May Alcott's *Little Women*. (Of course, I was Jo.) As we departed, we wound our way down the wooded drive, away from the house and away from an afternoon that is now a treasured memory of a timeless tea.

Tidbits

The following tantalizing tidbits are a sampler of the delectables served during teatime at Mrs. Bell's Tea Parlor, which is part of the Forest Farm Bed & Breakfast in my hometown, Brighton, Michigan.

Pound Cake with Lemon Curd

3/4 lb. butter, softened

4 oz. cream cheese, softened

1 1/2 c. sugar

3 large eggs

3/4 t. vanilla

1 1/2 c. all-purpose flour

1/8 t. salt

Preheat oven to 300 degrees. Grease and flour 4 mini-loaf pans. Line bottoms of pans with waxed paper cut to fit.

Beat butter and cream cheese at medium speed 2 minutes or until creamy. Gradually add sugar, beating 5 to 7 minutes. Add eggs, one at a time, beating until yellow disappears. Add vanilla, mixing well.

Combine flour and salt. Gradually add to butter mixture, beating at low speed just until blended. Pour into mini-loaf pans.

Fill a 2-cup glass measuring cup with water and place in the oven with the cakes. Bake at 300 degrees for 1 hour or until a wooden toothpick inserted in the center of a loaf comes out clean. Cool 15 minutes. Remove from pans. Serve with lemon curd.

(English Provender lemon curd is a Forest Farm favorite. English Provender strawberry and raspberry curd are also wonderful.)

Cream Scones

2 c. all-purpose flour
1/4 c. sugar
1 T. baking powder
1/4 t. salt
1/3 c. cold butter, cut into pieces
1 c. whipping cream
2 T. whipping cream or 1 egg white
1 t. orange zest
1/2 c. currants, dried cherries, dried cranberries (optional)
1/2 c. chopped pecans or walnuts (optional)

Preheat oven to 375 degrees. Combine flour, sugar, baking powder, and salt with a pastry blender until the consistency is course and crumbly. Add 1 c. whipping cream, stirring just until moistened. Option: Add 1/2 cup currants, dried cherries, dried cranberries, chopped pecans or chopped walnuts as you stir in the whipping cream.

Turn out onto a lightly floured surface, knead 5 or 6 times. Roll until 1/2-inch thick. Cut with a round biscuit cutter and place each scone about 2 inches apart on a nonstick baking sheet.

Brush the tops of the scones with the remaining 2 tablespoons whipping cream or egg white. Sprinkle the tops with sugar.

Bake at 375 degrees for 15 minutes or until golden brown. Yield: 1 dozen.

Serve scones warm with Devonshire cream, jam, and lemon curd.

Chicken Cashew
Dainty Tea Sandwiches

∾

1/4 t. Dijon mustard

1/4 t. salt

black pepper to taste

1 T. olive oil

1 T. white wine vinegar

10-oz. can white meat chicken (in water)
   or cooked chicken, diced

2 hard-boiled eggs (optional)

1/4-1/3 c. mayonnaise

1/4 -1/3 c. sour cream

1 t. capers

1 T. chopped parsley

1 t. chopped dill

1/8 t. Mrs. Dash's herb and garlic
   seasoning

1/4 c. chopped cashews

2-lb. loaf homemade white bread

In a large mixing bowl, whisk together mustard, salt, pepper, olive oil, and vinegar. Add diced chicken and refrigerate for at least one hour. May refrigerate overnight, if desired.

Finely chop the hard-boiled eggs. Mix with mayonnaise, sour cream, capers, parsley, and dill. Stir egg mixture into marinated chicken. Add Mrs. Dash's seasoning and cashews. Taste, add more salt or pepper, if desired.

Spread onto homemade white bread to the edges. Trim crusts from sandwiches. With a sharp knife, cut trimmed sandwiches into quarters and cut quarters again to form triangles.

Makes 10-12 sandwiches. Prepare approximately one sandwich per person.

Devonshire Cream

A wonderful complement to cream scones and jam! Should you find yourself not on the milk lorry route from Devon, here is an American version of England's famous Devonshire or clotted cream.

1 3-oz. package cream cheese, softened
1 T. sifted powdered sugar
1/2 t. vanilla
1/3-1/2 c. whipping cream

Beat cream cheese until light and fluffy. Beat in sugar and vanilla. Gradually beat in enough whipping cream to form a mixture of spreadable consistency. Do not over-beat. Cover and chill 2 to 24 hours. Makes 1 cup.

Traveling Teacups

I was on an extended road trip, speaking and traveling alone, when I stopped at a friend's home for a one-night respite. Being with people who care seems to breathe life back into a weary soul.

I arrived at Todd and Lauren Hess's home late and climbed into a beautifully prepared bed. I immediately slipped into a restorative sleep. When I awoke in the morning, I was greeted by my hostess delivering a tray to my bedside. Her cheery presence was like sunshine on a pillow; it warmed me.

On my tray was a fresh-brewed cup of tea with my breakfast. The fragrance from the tea settled around me like a down comforter. I cozied down into my environment and basked in the cordial care I was receiving. Lauren's tender mercies were especially meaningful after having been in a series of hotels. (There is nothing like contrast to increase our gratitude.)

Touch is healing and, yes, necessary to the human heart. Whether the touch is administered in the embrace of a welcome, the offering of refreshment, or the extending of solace, it soothes our souls. This realization from my own experiences led me to encourage women's groups to incorporate a Special Moments ministry in their churches.

Special Moments is not only the name of a delightful tea, but it is also what occurs over tea as women reach out heart-to-heart and touch each other's lives. Some of the most significant changes in my life have occurred after meaningful conversations with other women, women who have offered me the value of their insights and the safety of their acceptance.

Actually, you don't have to have a group to experience special moments. What you will need, though, is two teacups, two tea bags tucked in a small basket, and a destination. Perhaps you know of someone who would love to see you, but you just haven't taken the time to stop by. Well, today's the day.

Tap on her door and ask if she has thirty minutes (or less) for a special moment. If so, you take in your basket and ask if she would heat some water. Then set out the cups and bags, pour in the water, and convey your interest in how she is doing. Then you listen. After twenty-five minutes, you empty the cups, tuck them back in your basket, thank the woman for sharing a special moment, hug her, and scoot out the door.

Note two important guidelines: One, if you haven't forewarned your friend of your arrival, then ask before you enter if this is a good time for her (don't assume). Two, tell her up front about the abbreviated visit time. That allows her to have a fair expectation and frees you both to move on with your day.

In this busy world, if you don't purpose to have a special moment, it will slip past you. If you're like I am, you keep waiting for a big block of time to enjoy an extended chat before you commit to a visit. But that time never seems to materialize because life's dailyness keeps invading our plans.

If your church has a women's ministry, try setting up Special Moments teams.

You can be a real source of encouragement by sending out teams of two to visit women in their homes. Make sure they take teacups and tea bags. And be as creative with your baskets as you would like, including doilies, candles (bring matches), sugar cubes, and tea cookies. This takes the pressure off the woman who otherwise could end up scurrying about trying to figure out what she can offer you. Don't make it complicated by bringing too much, though, because then the preparation and execution take up too much time and become counterproductive. Simplicity, availability, and brevity are keys to an effective outreach. It's an opportunity to say, "I'm thinking about you and care about your world."

We all, at times, want to stop our world and get off, whether it's for a night or for thirty reflective moments. Brief reprieves can give us the momentum to reboard life and travel on.

Dear Lord,

May we remember how important it is to ask and to be asked, "How are you?" and then actually to let someone tell us. May those who ask be wise enough to put time-boundaries on our answers (lest we bore them to death) and may we be astute enough to speak of what truly matters. Amen. ❧

Tiny Tea

Somersaults, soap bubbles, barrettes, tutus, and tea parties comprise a visual primer of a little girl's world. Girls skip, hopscotch, tiptoe, and cuddle. They are full of lilting giggles, sassy pouts, innocent schemes, and peppermint dreams. Little girls adorn themselves in mud streaks and Momma's lipstick in such a stylish manner as to win the coveted title "Princess." They charm their daddies' hearts and cause grown men to part with their fortunes to purchase them ribbons, kittens, roller skates, and dollies.

No, I don't have a little girl, but I *is* one! Through and through. Even though I can't skip as easily as I once did, my heart does. And I still take great delight in the tiny treasures of childhood.

One summer when I was a child, our family visited Uncle Virgil, Aunt Alma, and Cousin Ann. They had moved to the little town of Madisonville, Kentucky. I don't remember anything about their house except for one item on their premises, and that one thing I will never forget. It etched itself permanently into my memory.

Standing in their backyard was Ann's very own playhouse. *Did you hear me?* Her own, free-standing, window-adorned house. I was awestruck. That someone in my family would have a personal playhouse seemed incredible. I thought only Shirley Temple had that kind of good fortune.

That playhouse allowed Ann to entertain her dollies and girlfriends with endless parties. Imagine that. I did, for *years*. I pictured myself as the reigning hostess known throughout the neighborhood, if not the world, for my gala tea parties. After all, a playhouse showcases dress-up and pretend in such a fitting way, don't you agree?

One can, of course, pull off a memorable celebration without the grandeur of a playhouse. That's when imagination comes into play. In fact, my childhood imagination allowed me to have an even more expansive and elaborate playhouse than my cousin's. Not that I would have objected if someone had stepped into my make-believe world and given some tactile reality to my pretending. Actually, I imagined that, too.

With these memories in mind, it seemed fitting that a few years ago I should invite a young lady to join me for a tea experience. I thought it would be grand fun to give some little girl what I had dreamed of.

I first casually mentioned to five-year-old Tristen that one day we would have a tea party. For months following, whenever she would see me, her eyes would light up, and she would remind me of my invitation.

Finally the special day arrived. I set up my dining room table with tablecloth, teapot, my grandmother's dishes, and candlelight. Surrounding the table were several dolls and a couple of stuffed animals positioned on booster chairs to join us for cookies and tea.

FACING PAGE:

A menagerie of tea pals surround a Tom Thumb teapot and an elephant teapot that belonged to my husband's grandmother. (Note me in tutu—giggle!)

Tristen's eyes expanded as she surveyed our tea table. She had brought her doll, which formerly belonged to her Momma. When Tristen spotted my dolls gathered around the table, she suggested hers should join us. I quickly accommodated her, and we prepared for tea.

Tristen and I decided on Kool-Aid tea for our party. I assembled finger sandwiches to go with our exceedingly sweet beverage. Then I served the colorful menagerie of stuffed friends, placing cookies on each doll's and animal's plate.

I had an animated chat with Tristen's doll as I circled the table. Tristen watched me carefully. Then I sat down and picked up my cup. Tristen leaned toward me, nodded in the direction of her doll, and whispered in a grown-up voice, "She's not real."

"I know," I assured her.

I saw relief flood her eyes as her smile came back. I giggled heartily to myself. Tristen wanted to play make-believe, but only with someone who understood it was just pretend. I guess I was too convincing.

After tea we played with Muffy bears. (Muffys are sweet little dress-up bears with lots of costumes.)

Then Tristen had to leave for her half day of school. As she headed for her parents' car embracing her doll and Muffy, I wondered which of us had had the most fun.

I had thought I was putting on the party for Tristen, but in retrospect it may have been for me.

No, I don't have a little girl, but I is one!

Today is my tea party
"No gifts," my momma said.
"It is enough to have friends,
 a warm house and a bed."

(But if you should forget
and bring me some candy,
I wouldn't mind at all—
that would be quite dandy.)

See, Momma has forgotten,
when she was my size,
how it cheers a little heart
to have a sweet surprise.

So bring your dollies, please,
and your puppy, if you like.
We'll sip our tea together,
and I'll let you ride my bike.

Tea Care

Into each of our lives enter individuals whom we will never forget. Some swirl in like whirlwinds while others enter like peaceful breezes. My nutritionist, Dr. Marcella Starr, has definitely been a breeze of peace for me.

Some years ago my health was fragile, so my friend Florence recommended I see her doctor. Problem was, I lived in Michigan and Dr. Starr lived in California. But on a speaking trip to that area, I decided to pay Dr. Starr a visit for an initial evaluation. I was immediately taken with her sensitivity and compassion. I think we always hope for a tender-hearted person to oversee our well-being, but those able and willing to invest so personally seem to be in rather short supply.

For me to make regular office visits, with us living on opposites sides of the country, didn't seem reasonable. Still, we thought it was no accident we had been brought together as doctor and patient. So Dr. Starr and I agreed to keep close tabs via telephone calls, the mail, and prayer. For years this strategy worked even though many times she wished I were closer so she could give me her optimum care. (I also continued to visit my M.D. in my hometown, sharing with each doctor the other's findings.)

Anytime I was in California to speak, I would stop by to see Dr. Starr. She would greet me with enthusiasm and sincere interest regarding my health. I soon learned Dr. Starr felt passionately that a person's lifestyle and relational choices should be as wise as one's food selections because both had a direct impact on one's health. Therefore, she advised me not only on vitamins, supplements, and teas but also on topics such as the need to give and receive forgiveness. We prayed together during office visits if she detected I was harboring a less-than-gracious spirit toward someone. Under her tender tutelage, I came to realize how right she was about relationships as well as food.

Then, on one of my speaking-event forays to California, I arrived quite ill. I called Dr. Starr for advice, but I didn't have time in my schedule nor the strength to go see her. In response to my need, she created a care package and had her husband deliver it to my hotel. The good doctor sent an array of vitamins and supplements and even included an electric teapot and several teas she felt would expedite my recovery. In a day when hometown doctors who pay house calls are obsolete, her willingness to hand-carry healing to my hotel was touching.

Dr. Starr is a proponent of herbal teas for their medicinal benefits. And I certainly have experienced overall improved health by following her counsel.

If you have sashayed around herbal teas because the flavor tends to be too mellow to spark your taste buds, you may want to rethink your position. Especially if you need a boost in your well-being.

Whenever possible, use bulk tea rather than tea bags. Measure two teaspoons per four-cup pot. Steep for twenty minutes, then strain well.

For colds and flu, while the tea is steeping, steep your feet. Yep, soak your feet in very warm water before going to bed. It gives your circulatory system a boost to fight on your behalf while you're sleeping. After soaking your feet, pat them dry, then immediately put on warm socks, crawl into bed, cover up, and drink your steeped tea—all four cups. This translates into your getting up and down during the night a few times, but the inconvenience is worth the healthy result.

Here are some other teas you might want to take a sip of:

Red clover

a blood purifier, which also can be helpful for sore throats.

Chamomile

calming to the nervous system and helpful for the stomach.

Peppermint

soothing to the stomach.

Elderflower and peppermint

(1 teaspoon of each for a four-cup pot)—colds.

Catnip and peppermint

(1 teaspoon of each for a four-cup pot)—colds and flu.

Valerian root

calming to frayed nerves.

Paul d'Arco

cleansing, a purifier.

Time-Share Teapot

⌒

Life is full of bounty, and as we share from what we have, value and benefits accrue in our friendships. It's as though sharing makes us benefactresses, not necessarily of material wealth but of emotional and relational well-being. I've noticed women in particular enjoy sharing. Perhaps that's because we have a strong desire to be involved in reciprocal relationships. We girls are often quick to share ideas, feelings, time, opinions, nurturing skills, listening ears, recipes, insights, and even secrets.

My childhood friend, Carol, and I take pleasure in being involved in each other's lives. At times, we find it great fun to venture off together on escapades. At other times, we each go in a different direction and then come back for a chatty confab, when we can catch up on our adventures and examine our respective treasure troves.

Carol and I are drawn to many of the same things. This is usually a joy; although a few times, it's felt more like a jolt. For instance, because we are both antique bugs, we can look through an entire shop only to end up wanting the same item. Or shop separately only to discover we have duplicated our purchase. Or find ourselves desirous of the other's treasure. Such as … our time-share teapot.

Carol had joined a troop of her friends on a shopping outing and had discovered a petite, antique teapot that she just *had* to own. A few days later when I visited her home, she brought out the chubby little pink pot for my perusal. Well, I loved it. It was adorable. And, of course, I, too, wanted it.

I tried bribing, bartering, and bullying (not really), but Carol wouldn't budge. I reminded her of every sacrificial thing (all two of them) I had ever done on her behalf. She held out and held onto her prided pot. Or her potted pride. Well, anyway (sniff), I didn't get the pot.

April arrived and with it my birthday. How surprised and pleased I was when I opened my present from Carol, and the little pink pot was nestled inside the box. I squealed with delight. But then I felt wretched.

"No, I can't take this teapot," I heard my guilt-ridden self say.

"Yes, you can," Carol stated, sounding like a woman who had made up her mind.

This set us off on a verbal tug-of-war full of nos and yeses. Then a creative flash struck me. "Why don't we *share* the teapot?" I offered. "I'll keep it for a couple of months, and then you can have it for a few months."

Smiles wreathed our faces as we realized with this solution we would both win. And we have. The little teapot adorns her home for awhile and then mine. Carol and I have been pretty loosey-goosey about our visitation rights. Every once in a while we just willingly relinquish custody.

Exchanging the little teapot has caused a big stir. It's stirred up friendship and love as we share the bounty entrusted to us.

Tickled

❦

My friend Kay Garrett was born to do tea. Kay is charming, hospitable, and as lovely as a bouquet of calla lilies. (The calla lily is an elegant, show-stopping, ivory flower fit to be a chalice for a queen.)

I have stayed in Kay's home many times over the years, and my senses experience ecstasy whenever I have the pleasure of being her guest. Kay has a gift for details, finishing touches, and welcoming friends.

For instance, I know, when I enter her guest bedroom, a bed tray adorned with teapot, teacup, selected reading material, and flowers (her specialty) will greet me. Candy will be at my bedside, and a hand-scripted welcome note will rest on my pillow. Kay's handwriting is exquisite with flourishes in all the right places. And her choice of note cards always reflects friendship.

The bed is clustered with a dozen pillows in varying sizes and shapes. Each one is decorated in either florals, stripes, eyelet, or Battenberg lace. The pillows demonstrate the Garretts' desire to soften my journey. The guest bath is beautifully arrayed, providing for any need that might arise.

Kay also plans innovative outings for us, which always include tea. We have had tea parties at Kay's home or that of our mutual friend Connie. We have done hotel teas, tea rooms, and once we even had tea in a castle.

At Connie's home, we had a progressive tea that started on the front terrace, then moved into the garden room, eased into her dramatic dining room, slipped into her artsy kitchen, and ended (boo) on the back deck with a mountain view and a two-story, cascading waterfall (ahh).

Another time I accepted an invitation to speak at a retreat at Glen Eyrie Castle in Colorado Springs. To my added delight, Kay and Connie attended. The castle halls were like a labyrinth, with stairwells ascending and descending at every turn. I felt like a royal sleuth as I ribboned around the hallways to search out Kay and Connie's room for a chat. The first thing they did upon my arrival was to serve me tea, as we reveled in our palatial surroundings.

On yet another excursion, Kay, her two granddaughters, Crystal and Candace, and I completed a brisk shopping trip by treating ourselves to lunch at the Rose Tea Room.

The girls were young, five-ish and seven-ish, and I thought they would be bored-ish with our grown-up choice. After all, tearooms tend to be a little more formal—in fact, downright stuffy, when compared to, say, the place sporting the arches, with the indoor playground.

Imagine my surprise and delight when Kay's youngest granddaughter leaned over to her grandma and said, "Isn't this place just too cute? Don't you just love the napkins? And did you notice the lovely pictures on the wall, Grandma? May I have my own teacup? I love this place."

I was so tickled at her spontaneous response that I thought I would have to excuse myself from the table to giggle. Crystal's animated face and her spill of enthusiastic words blessed my heart. I don't know why I was surprised at this little lady's reaction. She was born to do tea, just like her Grandma Garrett.

Grandma's influence must have pressed an indelible teacup on both girls' hearts. For when it came time for Candice's tenth birthday, her grandmother arranged for the two of them to sip tea in the ornate Brown Palace hotel lobby in Denver. The Brown Palace is a landmark in the city and a beautiful Victorian structure. The large lobby's vaulted ceiling is lavishly trimmed in gold, and lush, upholstered chairs are arranged in conversational groupings. Candice relished every minute of her high tea experience, including the harpist's lovely renderings and the nosegay Candice's grandmother had created for her to carry to the event. The nosegay became a birthday tradition, as did the tea celebration.

When each of the girls turned twelve, their tea parties turned a bit more sophisticated. As a matter of fact, just last week Crystal had her twelfth birthday, and Kay took her granddaughter on a mystery tea adventure. They flew to Southern California and attended a tea with Mary Poppins at Disneyland. The program was replete with mini-musical and photos with Mary.

What fun that must have been, like stepping into a storybook to join the characters. Now that's something I've always wanted to do. How about you?

How fortunate we are to have the opportunity to imprint good taste in the lives of the young, to expose them to genteel atmospheres full of feminine nuances. In a day with so much gender confusion, how nurturing to offer little girls a time for dress-up and teacups.

If you don't have a little girl in your life, find one. Perhaps annually you could enlarge the circle of your influence to include a little girl. I promise you, you'll be tickled.

Tepid Tea, Please

❧

Imagine a graceful Limoges teacup … minus the handle. Now picture picking up the cup full of steaming liquid. Ouch!

Tepid is not usually an appealing temperature, but prior to cup handles, namby-pamby warmth protected delicate fingers from hot spots, not to mention spills. Tea originated in the Orient, and so did teacups. While many Oriental teacups remain handleless (though much thicker than our translucent china), the mid-eighteenth century English lady found the original cup design created awkward if not dangerous situations. Then, voilà, the teacup handle appeared, to end the dilemma and to allow us to extend and curl our pinkies while sipping our favorite tea.

Of course, teacups are not the only containers which, when full of a boiling concoction, can become too hot to handle. I'm that way when I am too full of myself and become displeased with something or someone. Containing and retaining frustration is the beginning of a bitter brew that can soon spill out on others. No one likes to pick up a delicate teacup only to find the beverage dangerously hot. The same is true with people.

The phrase, "I don't have a handle on it," implies someone facing difficulty and groping for a solution. Having a place to get a grip gives one a feeling of greater safety and control.

My papaw (grandfather) got a handle on his hot tea by pouring it into a saucer to allow it to cool. Sometimes, to expedite the process, he would blow cool drafts of air over the steaming liquid. Perhaps that is what we need to do when we feel overwrought—pour out our anger in an appropriate place (before the Lord, to a trusted friend) so we can cool down. Others' wise counsel can be like a cool breeze to our feisty disposition. Plus the cooling-off time can give us a much-needed handle on our responses. Once emptied of our contentious spirit, we then have more space for the Lord and can offer ourselves up to others as a cup of refreshment.

While it isn't wise to act out of emotional heat, spiritual zeal is the right temperature to please the Lord and to promote personal growth. The Lord makes strong statements about tepid faith being highly displeasing to Him, and

He cautions us that it's better for our faith to be either hot or cold rather than sickeningly lukewarm (Revelation 3:15,16).

One good way to turn up our spiritual burners is to develop a passion for Scripture. The Word will act as a handle for us in this topsy-turvy world so we can maintain our grip.

Need a starting place? Pour yourself a hot cup of tea and open your concordance to the following "t" words: *taste, thirst, truth,* and *tears.* Look up the verses, then allow the Holy Spirit to set your heart ablaze.

Tea Totes

About Sizes and Shapes

I enjoy my teapots much as I enjoy people—diversified. I would no more want my friends to behave alike than I would want my teapots to replicate each other's appearance. Variety in sizes and shapes offers intrigue, interest, and individuality.

My two-hundred-year-old Chinese teapot holds intrigue. Hand-carried from the Far East and older than our Declaration of Independence, the pot delights me. At the same time, my bird-adorned teapot is only seven years old, yet it sparkles with interest. Two bluebirds (my favorite feathered friend) perch atop this cheery pot as if to offer you a sweet song with your refreshment [see photograph on page 13]. The pot must be handled gently because of the fragile, dimensional grasses in the design. This delicate teapot will be a delight to behold for a long time.

My friend Eleanor gave me an individual (one-cup), silver teapot that had belonged to her mother. I had admired it on a visit to Eleanor's home, and when I had returned to my house, a package arrived from her. It was the precious little pot. I was ecstatic. She also had included two old floral cups that did not fare as well in their travels. When

I picked up the package, I could hear shards of china clinking. My heart sank. But my husband, Les, was able, with his trusty, fast-fix glue, to put the china puzzles back together, and now the cups are displayed on my windowsill. The silver pot, with its petite individuality, sits on a crochet-covered wicker tray surrounded by antique books.

We humans are also rare pots, aren't we? We are full of intrigue, as we each hold our very own history. Like the Chinese pot, some of us have experienced more of life than others. For example, my friend Flo is eighty-three years old. She swims laps at the local pool, collates her church's bulletins, writes the church's correspondence to the sick, maintains the church's flowers, is the gardener for the Forest Farm Bed & Breakfast, works on handicrafts for missionaries, crochets, and creates stained-glass pieces. I find Flo inspiring and intriguing.

Like the bluebird teapot, my friend Eva is a delight to behold. As a teenager, Eva was in a car accident that left her a paraplegic. Even though she sits in a wheelchair, she's taller than most people I know. Being with her leaves you breathless with the beauty of God's grace. When she shares her story, audiences weep, not in pity, but in amazement, for Eva exudes a sweetness that touches something deep inside others. And she sings like a bird, leading people into praise. I find Eva remarkable and interesting.

Is it just my opinion, or are most women who are packaged petite also feisty? Perhaps that happens to us from being overlooked, stepped on one too many times, or jostled about like a piece of mail. Or maybe, just maybe, our Maker knew we would need an inner advantage to make up for our wee outer casing. Whatever the reason and whatever our pot size, when feisty is offered up to the Holy Spirit, it can become dynamic sterling of the finest kind, just like my petite, silver tea tote.

It's the individuality that I find so highly inviting.

About Spouts

I was told to pay close attention to the location of the spout on a pot to determine its function. The spouts that are positioned low, close to the table, are for serving coffee. When a spout is located mid-pot, it's for tea. And a spout that is even with the lid is a chocolate pot. There are always exceptions to the rule, but the spout site is a helpful indicator.

Speaking of spouts, have you ever made what you thought was a great deal only to find out later that you were taken? Of course you have. Me too. Les and I bought what we thought was an antique chocolate set (high spout) only to find out it was brand new. It's still a lovely set, but since it was sold to us in the guise of an antique, our pleasure in it has been tempered.

I wanted to return to the store and "chat" with the owner, but that wasn't possible. For weeks when I would pass the set on my buffet, I would think what I would have said to the deceptive man given the opportunity. Talk about a spout … I'm afraid I have one. When I'm brewing, watch out!

"The mouth of fools spouts folly" Proverbs 15:2b warns us. Scripture also reminds us, "The mouth of the righteous is a fountain of life" (Proverbs 10:11a).

I'm grateful I couldn't get to that man who misrepresented his product lest with my words I misrepresent my Lord. I want what pours forth from my mouth to be life-giving.

I guess I'll have to have regular site checks on my spout to make sure I'm functioning as originally designed.

Dear Potter,

We realize we have been jarred by life, causing brokenness. Some of us feel like shards of china instead of the exquisite and intriguing vessels that we want to be. We want to be pots that, when poured, tipped, dropped, or spilled, issue forth streams of life. Please, You who rework clay to repair damage, mend us. In Jesus' restorative name, Amen.

Tuneful Tea

My toe taps and my heart sings when memories of high tea in the deep South fill my mind. My long-time friend Lana Bateman introduced me to tea Texas-style at the Adolphus Hotel. The Adolphus is a grand facility with the illustrious history of being the oldest hotel in downtown Dallas.

My first occasion to do high tea with Lana was for my birthday a couple of years ago. I knew when I stepped into the lobby that this would be an afternoon I would not soon forget. Beautiful floral arrangements, inviting furniture settings, lovely carpets, and an exquisite, one hundred-year-old grand piano created the initial ambiance.

Our pianist for the tea, Stephen, obviously loved playing the antique piano. Its baroque carving was only surpassed in beauty by Stephen's effortless playing of Bach, Chopin, Beethoven, Mozart, and Debussy.

A tea cart was rolled out for the presentation of approximately twenty different teas. We each chose our two favorites. I was drawn to a blackberry fruit and a spicy Oriental. The teas were prepared, and two steeping teapots were set before each of us.

Tea sandwiches brought oohs and aahs: salmon, blackened chicken, and egg salad delighted our taste buds. Then came scones with creamed butter and luscious strawberries. Next was a series of the most pleasing mini-pastries: mandarin cheesecake, hazelnut caramel cake, swan-shaped puff pastries, eclairs (my favorite), chocolate pecan pie, fresh fruit tarts, and tiramisú. The eating experience was climaxed with dark, light, and white chocolate truffles. Oh, my, what an extravaganza of food, tea, and fine music!

The hotel invites guests to attend the tea any time between the hours of 3:00 and 5:00 P.M. Lana and I found once we arrived, we didn't want to leave until we had emptied our teapots, tasted a wide range of the goodies, and heard Stephen play his parting piece. For us, the music was every bit as delicious as the food.

The tea experience and the music lingered on in our minds long after our Adolphus visit. Actually, make that "visits." Yes, we returned, and we are planning to have future tea experiences. In fact, Lana has given a Tuneful Tea as her birthday gift to many of her friends.

There is nothing like friendship and tea. They're even better than eclairs. I treasure being able to share with those I love that which is pleasing. But even if Lana and I had to sip our tea from tin cups in a desert, we would delight in one another's company. (Of course, we prefer the Adolphus.)

She and I have walked through some pretty rough seasons together, including financial ups and downs. But we have learned no tea is as sweet as friendship. Each friendship can be sweetened with time together over tea.

So whether you plan a high tea in your Sunday Goin'-to-Meetin' clothes or low tea on a front porch step in your blue jeans, whether you sip from bone china or a mason jar, whether you're eating tiramisú or a Twinkie, whether you're listening to Bach or the Beach Boys, the important thing is to make time for others and to enjoy the harmony of a fine-tuned friendship.

Tea and Flowers

Hollyhock laughter
Daisy delight
Potter's red building
Blossoms upright
Riotous roses
Tangled and tall
Embracing the gardener
Summer and fall
Half-door enclosures
Cherry bejeweled
Outfitted benches
Vased and tooled
Tea iced in pitchers
In sweet array
Violets on windows
A flower-filled day.

Tea-totaller

❦

Since Carol and I spend a great deal of time together, we often become involved in the same projects. And so it was with our teapot mania. That spell occurred when we both decided to add to our teapot stock by collecting Hall China teapots. We had noticed in our antique travels that Hall offered some interesting choices. We thought we would try to collect as many different ones as we could find. What we didn't realize was there is almost no end to this company's wares.

Hall China was established in 1903 in East Liverpool, Ohio. The company went from father to son and boomed in the 1930s and 1940s. The old china is especially collectible, but Hall China remains in business today.

We found many sizes of teapots by Hall, not to mention different shapes and colors. There were solid-colored, dotted, leafed, starred, banded, and silhouetted teapots, and teapots with birds, vegetables, or florals painted on them, often with accessories. Some

FACING PAGE:
The Hall teapots are displayed on my 1907 Hoosier. The Aladdin teapot was Les' grandmother's.

had full sets of dishes and even matching tea towels, bread boxes, and canister sets. Hall had designed a number of its pieces for companies (such as Westinghouse, Kraft, Jewel Tea, Sears, and so on) and for hotels. They made miniature twin tea sets, tea-for-two sets, and tea-for-four sets. Hall designed two-cup cube teapots; Aladdin lamp-shaped teapots; bowling ball-shaped teapots; automobile-shaped teapots; donut-shaped (honest) and double-spouted, dual-compartmented teapots. Some of the pots had built-in strainers, infusers, and metal covers to retain heat. They made Victorian, art deco, and musical teapots, as well as many other styles.

Yikes! Can you see our dilemma? Carol and I were in over our spouts. We would have to add wings onto our homes to hold our collections if we didn't come up with a plan. Besides, these teapots, which once sold for $1.75, have inflated to the point you wonder how they keep from blowing their own lids. Actually, it was our husbands' lids we were concerned about if we continued to stuff our homes with this steamy collection.

You know, there's just something about the shape of a teapot that romances my heart. It so invitingly promises warmth and pleasing conversations. It's, well, it's hard to resist.

But Carol and I decided to select our favorite patterns and add gradually to our collections. Carol chose Rose White and Blue Bouquet, while I, the younger one (by ten days), couldn't make up my mind. So my husband chose for me. He liked the Silhouette. But I soon learned I'm far happier as a potpourri pot-finder than I am as someone working from a scripted plan. My teapot shopping style really falls under the category of "willy-nilly."

Both Carol and I have slacked off in recent years with our Halls because of work obligations (and the need to replenish our funds). But we chatted the other day, and all I can say is—watch out hubbies, we feel a spell coming on!

Tea Maker

Steeped in His Word

Infused with His love

Sweetened by His Spirit

Stirred from above.

Tea Therapy

Margret Zander's friendship has been therapeutic for me. Meg came into my life when I needed a friend and a mentor. I was twenty-nine years old; she was forty-three and everything I wished I was but, quite honestly, wasn't. An exceptional cook, farmer (of crops and critters), goal setter, seamstress (professional), and nurturer of people, Margret's zest for life radiates through her sparkling laughter and delightful sense of humor.

At the time Meg and I became friends, I was battling depression, overwhelmed by life, and floundering physically and emotionally. For me to be around Meg was comparable to taking a mood elevator to the top floor. She buoyed my spirits and, by her example, bolstered my courage.

I remember Meg's merciful involvement when Jason, our second son, was born. This baby had colic. Need I say more? Those of us who have had colicky children (and survived) all qualify for heroism awards. Les and I were worn to a frazzle trying to comfort this child who couldn't be consoled. We would start off feeling sorry for our baby and end up feeling sorry for ourselves. When our strength was depleted, we would bundle up Jason and take him to the Zander home. Don't you just know they were thrilled?

Upon our arrival, Margret would fix Jason a baby bottle of peppermint tea, and he would settle down ... for a while. When he would begin to fuss again, Meg and husband, George, would take shifts with us walking, bouncing, rocking, burping, and feeding him. Eventually Jason would fall asleep (hooray!) and we would all have a reprieve (finally!). Then we adults would drink the rest of the peppermint tea to soothe our tense tummies.

Meg had a bumper crop of peppermint growing underneath a dripping water faucet outside her sliding glass door. She would pull up a handful of leaves, crush them so they would release their flavor and fragrance, and drop them in the teapot. After it steeped, she would fill our cups and serve us slices of her homemade, multigrain, to-die-for bread.

Meg's bread was made from wheat and rye she purchased from local farmers. After allowing the wind to blow through the grain (to remove dust and chaff), she would place it on her kitchen table to remove the stones, then she would grind the prepared grain into flour. By the time the bread was baking, it was all anyone who walked into the kitchen could do not to rip off the oven door and scarf it up. (Excuse me, do women scarf?) I tried to restrain myself by remembering that the experience wouldn't be complete without a cup of her peppermint tea.

I learned from Meg that fresh-from-the-garden herbs are the most satisfying way to partake of herbal teas. The flavors are far more defined, and the steaming aroma is almost healing in itself. Growing your own mint is easy, but it can be aggressive, bullying other plants out of its way; so it needs to be kept hemmed in.

Not only are Margret's teas a comfort, so is she. Meg has a spacious heart for people—lots of people. Her gift of hospitality doesn't hinge on every nook and cranny of her home being dusted, but on the needs of the people who walk through her door. Many, the young and the old, the rich and the poor, the infirm and the vital, have walked through her door to make their way to the bountiful table of this generous woman. At Meg's table, there is always space for another plate. She has fed more people in a year than I have in my lifetime.

Many times Meg sat with me, her waif-like friend, while we sipped tea, mused on life, and watched each other's children grow. Other things were always growing around her house: flower gardens, vegetable gardens, chickens, puppies, peacocks, bunnies, and ducks. Meg always has a project going. From digging out her own fruit cellar, to butchering her own beef, to upholstering furniture, to plucking chickens, to designing quilted bedspreads, to baking hundreds and hundreds of holiday treats to share with others. (The incredible recipe following is a sample of her cooking abilities.)

Thank you, my therapeutic friend, that in the midst of your full life, you took time for tea … and me.

Crummy Cake

Cream together:
2 sticks butter
2 c. sugar
4 eggs

Add:
3-1/2 c. flour
1 c. buttermilk
1/2 t. baking soda
1/2 t. baking powder

Mix well. Pour into greased, round tube pan. Bake for 45 minutes at 375 degrees.

Cook in a saucepan, stirring constantly:
2 pkgs Dr. Oetcher vanilla pudding
  (a German brand, available in most grocery stores)
4 c. milk
4 T. sugar

Let cool. Cream 2 sticks of butter and stir in cooled pudding.

In frying pan, brown:
3 c. oats
2 T. butter
2 T. sugar

Cut cake into three layers. Spread pudding mixture between layers and over whole cake. Sprinkle cooled oatmeal over the cake. Crummy cake will keep up to six weeks refrigerated. The flavor is enhanced with age.

Tea Things

A ccessories knock me out. I love all the peripheral tea goodies that complement and set the stage for the real stars, the teapot and the teacup. Even though one can have tea without lace, silver, and dripper sippers, who wants to? Dripper sippers, you ask? See, already you're feeling deprived, as you should, since dripper sippers add pizzazz and practicality to the tea experience. Let's investigate some enhancers:

Tea cozy—Now, this is an accessory I can get wrapped up in. Well, actually it's to wrap the teapot in, like the pot's own sleeping bag. Cozies keep the tea at a toasty temperature and can be a snazzy-looking addition to teatime. My first cozy was aluminum with a Styrofoam lining. It did its job, but the visual effect was, well, blah. My next one was knitted. Pretty, yes—helpful, not particularly. Some cozies look like inflated pinafores while others are quilted, crocheted, or decorated with needlepoint. Select the one that lights your lamp, and you and your teapot will remain (uh-oh, here comes the obvious) *cozy!*

Tea trays—Trays are especially helpful when I'm serving individuals who are scattered about the house. A tray gives boundaries for sliding cups, saucers, spoons, and hot teapot. And, of course, cleanup becomes more expedient with a tray. It certainly beats the old pile-them-a-mile-high-and-watch-them-fly routine, which results from our attempts to carry more than our hands and arms can corral. Besides, a tray is such a fine finishing touch to a tea service.

We have Les' grandfather's trunk sitting in front of our couch—a nice, old-fashioned setting for presenting a tea tray to guests. Of course, there are those who prefer a …

Tea cart—I've always thought it would be nice to own one, but I haven't had the space. My friend Carol has a wrought-iron and glass tea cart in her spacious Victorian dining room. A generous bay window showcases the white, scroll-handled cart beautifully.

FACING PAGE:

My antique Limoges china is enhanced with tea accessories such as the infuser and dripper-sipper.

How convenient and even romantic it would be to prepare a two-tiered cart with tea things and goodies and to roll the presentation to guests. Hmm, I wonder if I moved my desk into the corner, put the end table in the loft, stored the lamp, then maybe, just maybe …

Muffineers—What are these? Actually, a muffineer is a sugar shaker. Usually a combination of sugar and cinnamon was used to sprinkle sweetness onto tea cakes. Shakers can be purchased brand new or as old as Methuselah (well, almost). The price range is as wide as the variety; some rare finds can exceed a thousand dollars. I purchased a green, Depression-era muffineer for ten dollars. But the one I really wanted was the dark cranberry, Victorian glass shaker ticketed at $325. Beauties are available that would be dazzling additions to any tea table. An old, lovely sugar shaker would make an enchanting gift (hint, hint) for the tea connoisseur.

Dripper sippers—I bet you thought I'd never get back to this one. A dripper sipper is an ingenuous item, and one I wish I had thought up. It's a small gizmo with a sponge on one end, a hook on the other, and a bird in the middle, all attached to each other with elastic bands. The bird perches on the teapot's lid, the sponge tucks under the lip of the pot's spout, and the hook fits around the handle. (If you're really confused now, you might want to check them out in the photo.) The bird keeps the lid on while you pour, the sponge catches any drips from the spout, and the hook is your securing agent to hold it all in place. Voilà, the dripper sipper!

I received my first dripper sipper from my friend Nancy, who remembers her grandmother using them when she was young. You have to hunt around, but dripper sippers are out there. I have never seen any old ones, but I have stumbled on new ones in gift stores from time to time. Birds are just one design. I've also seen bunnies and butterflies.

Tea things are my kind of things, and perhaps they are yours, too. If you, like me, have a cupboard full, then it must be time to pull them out and put them into service. If you don't have any, check some out. They will add a shake more personality to your tea times.

Thoughtful Tea

❧

I love surprises. Not the jump-out-of-the-closet-and-scare-your-liver-out kind but the I-have-something-special-for-you kind. I guess in that way I'm still a little girl. An unexpected gift delights me.

Often when I arrive at a speaking event, the group will present me with a welcome gift. Because I've spent so many years traveling and speaking, I've received a grand array of presents—from cards, balloons, baskets, flowers, pictures, poems, and needlework to books, jewelry, and glassware.

Many people have been generous to me through the years, but I'm still thrilled whenever I'm treated so kindly. I guess we can't wear out thoughtfulness, no matter how many times we extend it. And I find it reassuring when I'm on the road that someone has prepared for my arrival. It gives me a sense of being with friends even though we may have just met.

Recently, I spoke in Hawaii where I received my first leis. I was captivated by their beauty and the *aloha* spirit with which they were bestowed. One lei was especially exquisite. The young woman who made it presented it to me, and I could tell as she encircled my neck with the lei that this was a heartfelt gift. She had created it from beautiful, white, orchid-like flowers, rich with fragrance. Interspersed among these were intricate blossoms she had woven from tea leaves.

My lei caused a flurry of attention when some of the island women eyed it. They told me it was an honor to be given such a lei. Somehow I had sensed that, and I sat for some time afterward just tracing the contours of the tea-leaf flowers. I felt honored. *What a unique way for two women to share tea*, I thought.

Over the years, I've received all types of baskets. One looked just like a vine-covered cottage. Another came replete with party paraphernalia: hats, horns, and confetti. And one of my all-time favorites included an antique teacup and a pair of lavender gloves.

I remember the two young women who gave me the basket telling me they had spent a day hunting for gifts to place in it. How affirming to think they would take the time and effort to make my gift so special. If I had been with them, they couldn't have made better choices. The lip of the teacup is scalloped and trimmed in gold. The cup itself is covered in hand-painted pink roses with additional touches of gold filigree trailing down the scroll handle. Years later, the teacup and gloves continue to be thoughtful reminders of my journey.

Speaking of journey, I've decided when I'm old I'll wear leis and lavender gloves and sip my tea from gold scalloped cups. I'll spend my time browsing old bookstores and antique shops searching out thoughtful gifts for others. Hmm, on second thought, perhaps I should begin today.

Enrich someone's life; be thoughtful.

Tempo

I love the rhythms of the different seasons. For instance, autumn is my most energetic time of the year. I seem to have fresh snap, crackle, and pop, as I skip down my leaf-blown paths. My mind is cleared of its usual static, and I gear up for fresh challenges. My tea of choice for that season is robust in flavor.

Winter's song is one of contrasts, featuring notes of celebration and hibernation. Singing carols while cozied up to a warm fire and sipping fruity hot tea soothes my nostalgic heart. From "all is calm, all is bright" to "baby, it's cold outside," winter finds me boot-scootin' my way down snowy paths.

Spring is a sassy serenade. Her finest note is renewal. Intermittent bursts of sunshine mixed with daffodils and mint tea make me hopscotch down spring's puddled path. If ever there were a season full of promise, it's this Easter-lily time of year.

Summer is the more languid note on my seasonal scale. On sultry days I enjoy stretching out on a lounge chair or, better yet, swaying lazily on a green-slatted porch swing. Those are the moments for tall glasses of sweetened tea full of clinking ice cubes. That clinking is indigenous to summer. Summer often finds me sauntering down a path toward the nearest shady porch.

My southern heritage taught me to appreciate a porch, a swing, and a glass of iced tea. Raised in the north by my southern parents, my childhood vacations in Kentucky exposed me to genteel summers. Our relatives were all diligent people who rose early, worked hard, and rested well. Midday often brought a much needed sit-down break. Everyone congregated on the porch to rest those weary bones a spell and to sip tumblers full of cool tea. Then it was back to work until supper.

Supper in the south for my family was often a platterful of mouth-watering fried chicken. Nestled close by were billowing clouds of mashed potatoes, a "mess" of green beans and home-grown sliced tomatoes. Add to that baking powder biscuits and chilled pitchers with more sweetened tea. And dessert. Strawberry shortcake, peach cobbler, icy slices of watermelon, hand-cranked ice cream, and banana pudding with mile-high meringue were just a few ways my family topped off a meal. After the table was cleared and the kitchen was tidied up, it was back to the porch swing with—what else?—an enormous jug of tea.

Whiling away a summer evening in Kentucky is one of my favorite childhood recollections. As lightning bugs darted about in the dusk, the sounds of family members' visiting, their talk seasoned liberally with laughter, the rhythmic tones of the porch swing, creaking rockers, and tinkling ice comprise an unforgettable summer song in my memories. Because of my immediate family's limited opportunities to be involved in our relatives' holiday celebrations, birthday parties, and other significant events, those infrequent visits to the South are an especially fond remembrance.

Summer tea seeped into so many of those moments together. The jingling ice served as kind of a family bell to call us all together onto

AT RIGHT:
Mamaw and Papaw's shadded porch on their old Kentucky home.

covered porches, under shady trees, or surrounding the supper table. Those occasions allowed me to revel in family connectedness.

I not only loved interacting with grandparents, aunts, uncles, and cousins, but I also enjoyed watching them interact. They were a script that helped me understand more of who I was. And so, to my relatives, both past and present, I lift my glass of tea and wish for them continued paths full of sweet tempo.

Tumblers full of summer rays,
iced and sweet to taste.
Sipping deep of yesterdays,
childhood's mirrored face.

Shady spots along life's road,
a swing to sit a spell.
Time to write a family ode,
time to hear a bell.

Firefly's flickering torch
keeps my mind aglow.
Mamaw's Kentucky porch,
my twilight tempo.

Tradition

My friends Richard and Barbara Ott are world adventurers. They have traveled to places I've never even heard of and some I have, including to China, where they lived for several years.

After Barb adjusted to the different culture in Beijing, she began to venture out on shopping treks. No malls with vast parking lots here—Beijing offered limited slots for cars since the main mode of transportation is bicycles. Barb said cars were often parked on sidewalks because nothing else was available. (I've considered trying that myself.) Driving was slow and could be tedious in rush hour bicycle traffic. (Of course, because of the bustling population in China, almost every hour was rush hour.)

On one of Barb's visits stateside, I put in a request for a teapot when she returned to Beijing. And am I glad I did. Barbara brought me a pot of antiquity. In fact, she had to petition the government to be able to take it out of the country. Believed to be more

FACING PAGE:
Ancient Chinese teapot adorns my kitchen table.

than two hundred years old, the teapot had to receive a wax seal with the government's insignia for customs to allow it through.

I don't even dust my treasured teapot very often, lest I harm it. How would one replace such a gift? It's unlikely I'll bike over to Beijing anytime soon. Besides, when I'm that old, I don't want to be dusted anymore either. Just tip me over and pour me out.

Barbara told me she bought my pot at an indoor flea market that was next to the Temple of Heaven. As she walked from stall to stall she could have bought jewelry, clothing, furniture, pottery (templeware—yikes), clocks, opium pipes (double yikes), and teapots. I am grateful she opted for the teapot.

We would expect China to have a lot of teapots since tea is their national beverage. The traditional story on the origin of tea as a beverage goes something like this: Four thousand years ago, Emperor Shen Nung was having his water boiled before partaking of it. A gust of wind blew some wild tea leaves into the open pot. The taste was so pleasing to the emperor he had the bush cultivated; he added the beverage to his menu. The next thing you know, the Ritz in New York was offering high tea. (Okay, this is the abbreviated version of the evolution of tea.…)

In northern China, teacups look more like large coffee mugs. In the south of China the cups are smaller and usually without handles. The northern mug-style cups not only have handles but also lids. The teas are loose, and often the same leaves are used all day. Since the Chinese don't use strainers or tea bags, I wonder if they end up with leafy smiles, like I do with broccoli?

Regardless what cup I use to sip my tea, I feel fortunate to have such a unique teapot, full of tradition, in my collection. If I were a betting woman (which I'm not), and someone would ask me (which no one has) if I would ever own a teapot older than our country, why I would bet all the tea …

Table Toppers

❧

To watch my mom crochet was like observing a ballet of handiwork. Able to carry on involved conversations while she worked, Mom seldom dropped a stitch. With seemingly effortless hand movements, she created elegant table spreads, table toppers, and tablecloths. Her work has graced many a tea table, supper table, and side table.

Mom's favorite design was the pineapple pattern, also called the peacock pattern. Occasionally she would venture out and choose a different design, but she would quickly return to her pineapple passion.

And passion it was. Mom made countless pieces throughout the years but was unwilling to sell them at any price. She chose instead to bestow them as gifts to surprised recipients. Sometimes Mom gave them to strangers like a bank teller or store clerk for some kindness they had extended to her. She gave her crocheted creations as graduation gifts, wedding and anniversary gifts, and just-because-you're-in-the-family gifts.

A floor-length tablecloth would take several months of Mom's diligent effort, working each day for hours on end. And the result was exquisite. (Glimpses of her work are visible in a number of photos throughout the book.) I still feel honored, when I prepare for tea by dressing

my table in Mom's lovely handiwork. The tablecloth she made for me is truly an heirloom, and one I imagine my future grandchildren and great-grandchildren will use with pride for their special teas.

Today my mom can no longer crochet, but her meticulous handiwork continues to add beauty to our lives.

She selects wool and flax
and works with eager hands.

PROVERBS 31:13, NIV

Theme Tea

~⌢~

Themes bring a satisfying connectedness, whether it's "Lara's Theme" from *Doctor Zhivago*, a church retreat theme, or a decorating theme throughout a room. Like stitching a garment with the correct color of thread, a theme not only looks good, it also wears well. I have a number of thematic remembrances that, over the years, have continued to wear well in my memories. For instance …

Les and I lived at a Youth for Christ camp when we were raising our sons. Three other families resided on the grounds. The families decided to each host a theme dinner. Whatever theme was picked dictated the food choices, the decorating, and even the clothes we wore.

The Vaden family was first, and they chose a Japanese theme. We sat on the floor at low tables and ate with chopsticks while sipping hot tea from handleless cups. One guest, Karen, even had her mom ship her a kimono to wear for the evening.

When it was Karen's turn in March, her theme was Irish. The color theme for the decor and our attire was shamrock green and linen white. The tables were covered with beautiful linens from Ireland, and the beverages included a festive green punch. Green tea was served in fine white china cups.

Les and I took our turn in the summer, and I selected a southern theme partly because my Kentucky-born mom was living with us, and she makes the best southern fried chicken in the world. No, make that the universe. (Her recipe is so good—trust me on this—that chickens volunteer their legs just to be included.)

For fun, I equipped the bathroom, which sported a half-moon on the door, with old catalogs and corncobs. For trivets at the table, we used slabs off tree trunks. Some of our guests took advantage of the hot weather theme and came barefoot, with rolled-up bib overalls and straw hats. Our chicken, gravy, and baking powder biscuits were served with frosty tumblers of iced tea.

Yes, themes can make events more memorable. As I think back, I can almost see and taste the themes we chose; they are forever etched in my that-was-fun remembrances.

Another theme party I remember was when I put on a small, weekend seminar some years ago. I decided to surprise the ladies with a late-night tea party. After the evening session, the ladies went to their rooms, thinking it was time to retire. That's when the fun began.

I gave the women just enough time to slip into their pajamas, and then I sent a courier from room to room to deliver Sweet Dreams Tea Party invitations. The ladies came giggling to my door wearing their robes and rollers in their hair, wondering what was up. A friend and I put on a skit for them, and then we read to them a portion of the children's book, *The Velveteen Rabbit*. All the while the gals were partaking of Sweet Dreams tea that we had ready for them at the beginning of our party. (The tea bags came individually packaged in jackets with the Sweet Dreams name on them, which helped carry out our theme visually.) Following a good-night prayer, the ladies were sent back to their rooms to have—what else?—sweet dreams.

Do you have sweet dreams in your past? How about parties that wear well in your memory? Perhaps it's time (once again) to create some thematic moments and lasting memories.

Tender Tea

~

Isn't romance wonderful? On a cold evening, I so enjoy a blazing fire and watching a tasteful, romantic movie. Say, maybe, *Little Women*.

Remember when Jo finally meets the humble professor, but they are both so uncertain of the other's heart that they almost give up on their relationship? Then, at the end, we see Jo run after her one true love in the rain. Under the shelter of an umbrella, they express their feelings. Oh, sweet beginning love.

The only thing more appealing than beginning love is seasoned love, love with history. Tried and true, possibly trampled-yet-triumphant love is seasoned. When my grandfather died, my grandparents, Franklin and Thanie McEuen, had been married more than fifty years. *Fifty* years, the golden anniversary. They had to go through a lot of paper, wood, and tin years to reach the pure gold stage. During the unfolding of their days together, they stockpiled memories, shared hardships, forgave offenses, and deepened commitment.

When Thanie lost the love of her life, she carried on with dignity … and a lingering sadness. Could it be any different? For fifty years they had eaten together, talked together, and slept together. Then, suddenly, one was missing. Now who would romance her, if only to inquire about her headache and brush a tender kiss against her brow? Only Jesus and eternity could ease her underlying bereavement.

Romance for me is the tender inquiry, the well-placed word, the shared laugh, the spoken prayer, and the thoughtful embrace. It is time. It is gentleness. It is personal regard.

I've been married to Les for thirty-five years. He's a contradiction in some ways. (Aren't we all?) He's something of a rogue, mischievously playful. And he's also a tenderly thoughtful romantic. What a delightful combination! Les often catches me off guard by being bodacious and outrageous one moment and then suave and debonair the next. Don't tell him, but I wouldn't give up either part of him. Moderate one side or the other, perhaps. But give up? Never!

To be honest, my husband is more thoughtful than I am, although this has not always been so. Les came from a family that didn't find it easy to express tender feelings in spoken words. Instead, he has learned and grown into that kind of man during our marriage. And I have reaped the benefit of his loving journey.

Often Les surprises me with breakfast in bed. It's not an unusual sight in our home to see him carrying an antique oval wicker tray to my bedside. There he serves me cooked oatmeal (my favorite) in a flow-blue bowl, orange juice in a stemmed goblet, and raspberry tea in a china cup with a sterling spoon and a cloth napkin. Now *that's* romantic!

Girls, you can have your bangles and baubles. Just give me a man who's willing to make me a cup of tea. It's really not even the tea or the service, as lovely as those things are. For me, it's Les' desire to do something that pleases me. That makes me swoon.

Yep, fifty years with this 24-carat golden man will be no problem. It will be a piece of cake (wedding cake, of course).

Tranquilli-tea

‡

Have your emotions ever felt like a tangle of rubber bands that have been stretched past the point of elasticity? Well, that's how I felt when I arrived in Boston to speak to eight hundred women.

My hostess and the chairman of the group was Jan Carlberg. I had met Jan that summer at the Christian Booksellers Convention and had felt comfortable with her immediately. So when she invited me to speak at her church, I really wanted to. But by the time the date arrived, my life had gone awry.

In the midst of my demanding schedule, we had discovered my mom would require surgery for breast cancer. Then, after her release from the hospital, we planned an outing in which we would take her to church and out to dinner. In the restaurant, on our way to the table, Mom slipped on the tile and crashed to the floor, breaking her hip. Back to the hospital she went and back into surgery. I'm grateful that my mom has a lot of moxie.

During her surgeries and recoveries, I was darting back and forth across the country to speaking engagements. I felt like a hummingbird, flapping my wings as hard as I could. I'd buzz in, dash to the hospital, spend up to eight hours with Mom, see her doctors, run home to repack, and, after another visit with her, dart off to the airport again. Needless to say, after weeks of this pace I didn't feel or act too swift. I was exhausted, and now it was time for me to go to Boston.

As I flew into Massachusetts, I remembered from my school days that Boston was where they had the riotous tea party. Crates full of tea were dumped into the harbor. That sounded inviting. No, not the tea, but being slid into the harbor. There I could bob about aimlessly. I was so tired.

Jan met me at the airport and warmly embraced me. Her greeting encouraged my wayfaring soul. We arrived at her home where she invited me to rest while she ran errands. Rest. What a sweet offer. Rest. What a sweet sound. I climbed into bed and fell sweetly asleep.

That evening Jan gave me a choice of several dining experiences. I chose to eat at the ocean. We dined at a lovely restaurant across the street from the sea where twin lighthouses flashed hope in the distance. During dinner I mentioned the Scripture "The voice of the Lord is upon the waters" (Psalms 29:3). After our meal Jan drove to a pull-off next to the water and rolled down the windows. She smiled and said, "I thought you might like to hear His voice."

I couldn't begin to express how restorative that was to me. I felt the knots in my rubber-band emotions begin to untie. I leaned my head back, closed my eyes, and listened. Each wave that drew away from the shore seemed to take with it some of my weariness, and each incoming wave brought renewal. The ocean's rhythm spoke of God's tranquillity to my tense soul.

When we arrived back at Jan's home, she brought me a simmering cup of herbal tea for my bedside. That night I had the sleep of a child.

The next day Jan took me to The Wenham Tea House. This was my first visit to Boston, my first exposure to a bona fide tea room, and my first opportunity to sample clotted cream and lemon curd.

On my trip home, I was amazed I could have arrived so spent and then left, after speaking, so uplifted. Jan will never know how desperate my parched heart was, nor how God used her to serve me much more than tea.

Are you fatigued? Tied in knots? Perhaps you can't escape to the ocean, but let me suggest you brew some tea, fill the tub, and then dive in. Don't bob about, don't even pout. Just lean back and listen, " For the voice of the Lord is upon the waters."

Ascribe to the Lord the glory due to His name;

Worship the Lord in holy array.

The voice of the Lord is upon the waters;

The God of glory thunders,

The Lord is over many waters.

The voice of the Lord is powerful,

The voice of the Lord is majestic.

PSALMS 29:2-4

Tribute

❧

I feel blessed to have had women wealthy in character enter my circle of reference and make rich deposits in my life. One woman who has made a profound difference in me and for me is my mom, Rebecca Ann Meyers McEuen.

My mom is small of stature (4'10"), big in her beliefs, and expansive of heart. She is tender and easily moved to tears. Yet, as a child, I knew better than to mess with Mom by being disobedient, because she could grow really tall (maybe 7' 4"), if you crossed her. She was a diligent housewife, excellent money manager, and extremely generous. Mom was a Jacquelyn-of-all-trades, a truly handy gal to have around the house.

FACING PAGE:

*My mother, daughter-in-law Danya, and I
gather in front of my fireplace.*

Telling my mom she couldn't do something was like a dare … and she was always up to a dare. She had a great sense of humor, which she would lose only in the face of injustice. Mom was a cheerleader for the downtrodden. Her faith and her family were of paramount importance, and Mom would have taken on armies, if necessary, to protect both.

My mom could swing a hammer, sling hash, bring hope, ring true, and sing "How Great Thou Art." What she started, she finished, and did so well. She was a first-class plodder and steady as the Rock of her faith.

Gratefully, at the writing of this book, my mom, now eighty-one years old, is still living. Life has changed for her in many ways. Daddy is gone now, and I know her hand aches for his. They walked in tandem, but now his steps have stilled. When Mom speaks of him, her voice softens, and her eyes mist.

Many memories are now stored on shelves too high for her to retrieve. And while Mom's strides are slower, her determination reigns strong. She may have forgotten your face, but she continues to care about your heart.

Mom's aging body is a contrast to her young ways. Sometimes she hears music we can't, and I see her tap her toes to it. And I've noticed something else: She has become especially wistful at the name of Jesus.

To you, Mom, good soldier of the faith and lover of your family,
I lift my teacup in tribute.

I will extol Thee, my God, O King;
And I will bless Thy name forever and ever.
Every day I will bless Thee,
And I will praise Thy name forever and ever.
Great is the Lord, and highly to be praised;
And His greatness is unsearchable.
One generation shall praise Thy works to another,
And shall declare Thy mighty acts.

❧

PSALMS 145:1-4

Treasures

The day after their wedding, my parents, Smith and Rebecca McEuen, had this picture taken in a four-for-a-quarter photo booth. Sitting in the foreground of the photograph is a teacup my dad gave to Mom. Today it is one of my treasures.

Purple violet garden
on a yellow china cup.
Yesterday's reminder
as I sit down to sup
of Dad's love for Mom
in the prime of life
When he courted her,
and she became his wife.

Purple violet garden
memories from the past.
Blossoms bud today
while love's fullness lasts.
Cup of remembrance,
measure of time,
keepsake to treasure
of romance sublime.